P9-DHM-996

Shape
space

Shape Space

Cathryn Falwell

Clarion Books
NEW YORK

For the children of
Noah Webster School
Hartford, Connecticut

With grateful thanks to
Dinah Stevenson

Clarion Books
a Houghton Mifflin Company imprint
215 Park Avenue South, New York, NY 10003
Text and illustrations copyright © 1992 by Cathryn Falwell
All rights reserved.
For information about permission to reproduce selections from
this book, write to Permissions, Houghton Mifflin Company,
2 Park Street, Boston, MA 02108.
Printed in the U.S.A.

Library of Congress Cataloging-in-Publication Data

Falwell, Cathryn.
Shape space / Cathryn Falwell.
p.   cm.
Summary: A young gymnast dances her way among geometric shapes.
ISBN 0-395-61305-1
1. Geometry—Juvenile literature.   [1. Geometry.   2. Shape.]
I. Title.
QA445.5.F35   1992   91-32274
516'15—dc20   CIP
                                                      AC

WOZ 10 9 8 7 6 5 4 3 2 1

What's inside?

Is it for me?

Let me see!

Shapes!

toss them out
all about
through the air
big ones here
small ones there...

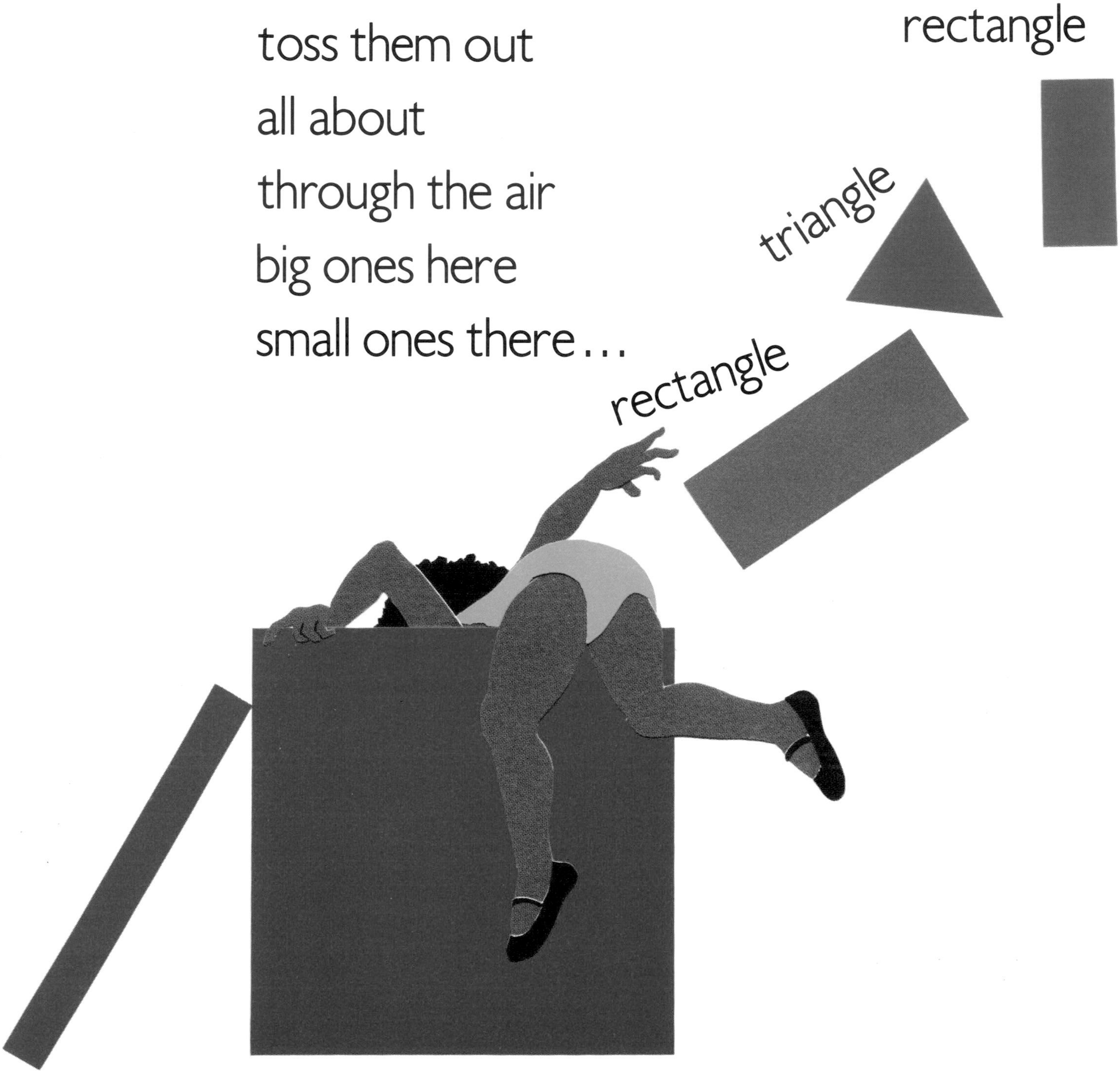

rectangle

triangle

rectangle

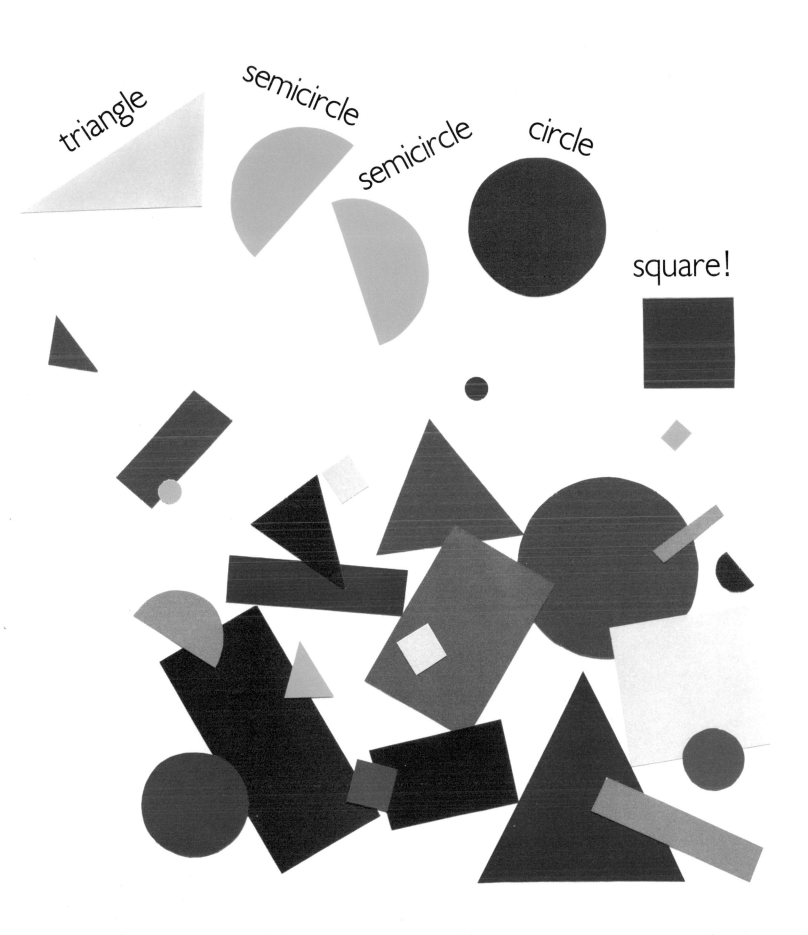

triangle

semicircle

semicircle

circle

square!

Hmmmm . . .

Hop on rectangle
rock on rectangle

flat on top

rock

rock

rock

rock on triangle

tap on triangle

tip on triangle

tilt on triangle

Semicircle
semicircle

down

to

the

ground

S w i n g

a circle round and round

Step
on square
stop
on square

s t o p !

Now,
stack them
high
to the
sky

Watch it grow . . .

Here we go

Rectangle, triangle, rectangle, triangle,

semicircle, semicircle, circle, square!

hat to wear?

Try on a
triangle . . .

hy not share?

Make a
friend . . .

Rectangle
triangle
rectangle
triangle
semicircle
semicircle
circle
square!

Take a
shape
take a
step

take a
chance
try a
dance . . .

Watch us
step
watch us
dance
in the space.
What a
pair!

Rectangle,   triangle,   rectangle,   triangle,

semicircle, semicircle, circle, square!

Shapes

up

shapes

down

dance all around

ow . . .

     rumble down rectangle
     tumble down triangle
     stumble down semicircle
     crumble down circle

       fall

         down

          square!

Time to stop.
toss them in
once again

big and small

and that's all....

Rectangle

triangle

rectangle

triangle

semicircle

semicircle

circle

square!

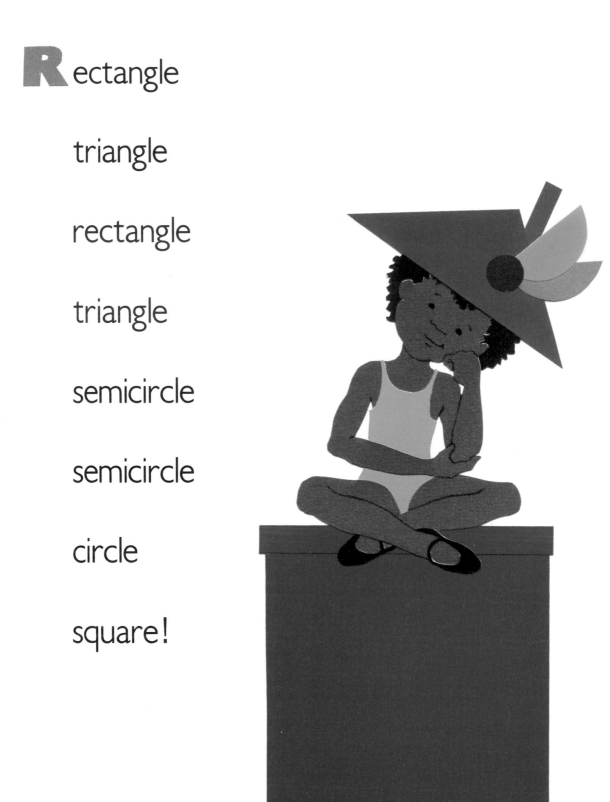